The manuscript chapters of
PERSUASION

THE JANE AUSTEN LIBRARY

The Jane Austen Library has been established to make available rare or otherwise unavailable editions of the novelist's work and of the most important biographical and critical studies. In particular, the Library will include the authoritative texts of the juvenilia and other smaller works and unfinished manuscripts originally prepared by Dr R. W. Chapman and issued by The Clarendon Press. All the volumes in the Library will carry a new Preface.

THE JANE AUSTEN LIBRARY

The manuscript chapters of PERSUASION

Jane Austen

Edited by R. W. Chapman

PR
4034
.P4
1985b
West

THE ATHLONE PRESS
LONDON AND DOVER, NEW HAMPSHIRE

This reprint has been authorized by the
Oxford University Press. Reprinted from the
Clarendon Press edition 1926 by permission
of the Oxford University Press

First published in this edition 1985 by
The Athlone Press Ltd
44 Bedford Row, London WC1R 4LY
and 51 Washington Street, Dover NH 03820

© Publisher's Preface and Foreword
The Athlone Press 1985

British Library Cataloguing in Publication Data
Library of Congress Cataloging in Publication Data

Austen, Jane
The manuscript chapters of Persuasion. – (The Jane Austen Library)
I. Title II. Chapman, R. W. (Robert William)
III. Series
823'.7[F]. PR4034.P4
ISBN 0-485-10502-0

Library of Congress Cataloging in Publication Data

Austen, Jane, 1775-1817.
The manuscript chapters of Persuasion.
(The Jane Austen Library; 3)
"Chapters 10 and 11 of the second volume as first
planned" – P. Reprint. Originally published: Two chapters
of Persuasion printed from Jane Austen's autograph.
Oxford: Clarendon Press, 1926.
1. Austen, Jane, 1775-1817 – Manuscripts – Facsimiles.
2. Manuscripts, English – Facsimiles.
I. Chapman, R. W. (Robert William), 1881-1960.
II. Title. III. Series: Austen, Jane, 1775-1817.
Jane Austen library; v. 3.
[PR4034.P4 1985b] 823'.7 85-6174
ISBN 0-485-10502-0

All rights reserved. No part of this publication may be
reproduced, stored in a retrieval system, or transmitted in any
form or by any means, electronic, mechanical, photocopying or
otherwise, without prior permission in writing from the publisher.

Printed in Great Britain at
the University Press, Cambridge

CONTENTS

Foreword Lord David Cecil	vii
Preface Brian Southam	xi
Preface R. W. Chapman	xv
Chapters 10 and 11 of the Second Volume as first planned	1
Facsimile pages	43
Notes	77

FOREWORD
by Lord David Cecil

Jane Austen does not seem to have taken either her works or herself over seriously. Certainly she showed no signs that they would be of interest to posterity. Yet now, after 150 years, she is one of the most popular of our classical novelists; moreover interest in her novels has begun to extend into interest in her. People want to know as much about her as they can, both as a writer and as a woman. The purpose of this Library is to do something to satisfy this want.

To take the writer first: the Library will include those of her writings that were not published in her lifetime; the skits and sketches she wrote as a child, already revealing her unique characteristic humour and turn of phrase; her one unpublished novel *Lady Susan;* the two books that she never finished *The Watsons, Sanditon;* also the last chapters of *Persuasion* in their first, afterwards discarded, form. All these in their different ways tell us much about her methods of work and her judgement as to when she thought she had succeeded and failed.

Next the woman. In this section we will find descriptions of her by people who knew her, in particular her nephews and nieces; she was the most delightful and loved of aunts. There will also be accounts of places she knew well, like Bath and Lyme Regis, and her relation to them.

The final section will consist of selected biographical and critical studies of her and her work by authorities in the subject.

The Library as a whole should expand and enrich our picture of Jane Austen, woman and novelist. A homogeneous picture; for the more we learn about her the more we discover that unlike many authors, the novelist and woman are of a piece. Knowledge of one throws light on knowledge of the other; and increases our delight in them both.

PREFACE
by Brian Southam

Dr Chapman's Preface points out that these two chapters are uniquely valuable to us as the only piece of manuscript to have survived from six novels; and his edition, in turn, is uniquely valuable in presenting us with a facsimile of the manuscript itself, as well as a transcription and textual Notes, so that we can follow every detail of the process by which Jane Austen rethought these crucial scenes in the novel. It is a display of the creative process that repays our closest attention and deepens our understanding of the author's aims and intentions in *Persuasion*.

Persuasion was written with speed, in almost exactly twelve months, between 8 August 1815 and 6 August 1816. On 8 July 1816 Jane Austen began the penultimate chapter, chapter 10 of the second volume. Eight days later, this and chapter 11, a draft of thirty-two pages, was completed. On the last page, she wrote 'Finis July 16 1816'. At once, she had second thoughts, erasing these words and writing an additional paragraph, followed by 'Finis July 18 1816'. At this time, she also wrote a passage of five hundred words to be inserted in chapter 10.

According to the *Memoir*, Jane Austen was unhappy with this ending: 'She thought it tame and flat, and was desirous of producing something better.' The problem seems to have weighed upon her until one morning, some days later, 'she awoke to more cheerful views and brighter inspiration: the sense of power revived; and imagination resumed its course'. The outcome was a new chapter 11, incorporating more than a quarter of the original chapter 10; and so the original chapter 11, with some small verbal changes, became the final chapter 12.

The author's dissatisfaction was with the way she had effected the reunion of Anne and Wentworth. In the original chapter 10 this was a comedy scene, with the Crofts cast as sly matchmakers and the lovers' feelings for one another brought to light through a series of blunders and upsets. In itself the scene is amusing and well-written. However, it clouds a major issue in the novel – Anne's fitness of mind and feeling to judge and override Lady Russell's objection to the marriage, the 'persuasion' which formerly kept her apart from Wentworth. The original version also fails to draw the intensity and depth of their love, nor do they come together with a full understanding of the past; whereas the new version shows their powers of self-determination, their control over their destinies and Wentworth's fitness for Anne. In contrast to the confusion and excitement of events which threw them together in the Admiral's house, at the White Hart there is an air of outward calm and spaciousness. The five people are carefully arranged about the room. The scene is highly pictured and through the observation of movement, speech, and reaction, we are kept fully conscious of the separate identities.

Henry James found the novels of Jane Austen 'instinctive and charming'. He advised readers to look elsewhere 'for signal examples of what composition, distribution, arrangement can do, of how they intensify the life of a work of art'. Yet, as the *Persuasion* manuscript reveals in the greatest detail, the inevitable rightness of the novel's conclusion was not, in the act of creation, a swift and effortless performance, but a triumph of rethinking won through trial and error. Here, if anywhere, is the evidence of that conscious art which James was seeking.

PREFACE

OF the novels published by Miss Austen no manuscript seems to have survived; and of *Northanger Abbey* and *Persuasion*, which were posthumously published in 1818, nothing survives except two chapters belonging to the last volume. The reason for their survival is plain. They were intended as the two concluding chapters of *Persuasion* and numbered 10 and 11; but Miss Austen, as is well known, was dissatisfied. She cancelled the greater part of Chapter 10, and substituted two new chapters, 10 and 11. The final chapter was retained (and became Chapter 12 [1]); but the surviving manuscript is not verbally identical with the chapter as printed. It is clear that she made a fresh copy of her final draft, and that it was the fresh copy that was sent to the printer. It

[1] In most modern editions it is called Chapter 24; the division into two volumes being obscured.

is clear, also, why she did so. In the surviving manuscript part of Chapter 10 was an afterthought, and was added at the end, after Chapter 11; the concluding chapter, therefore, was so embedded that it could not without some loss of tidiness have been removed.

The cancelled chapter was first printed by James Edward Austen-Leigh in the second edition (1871) of his *Memoir of Jane Austen*, (pages 167–180; see also p. 157). The final chapter has never been printed from this manuscript. Both chapters are here printed as Miss Austen left them when she laid aside this manuscript. In the notes are recorded

(1) all corrections and erasures which the editor has been able to decipher.

(2) in respect of the cancelled chapter, all verbal variations between the manuscript and the edition of 1871.

(3) in respect of the final chapter, all verbal variations between the manuscript and the edition of 1818.

PREFACE

The edition of 1871 was inaccurate in stating (p. 157) that Miss Austen "cancelled the condemned chapter, and wrote two others, entirely different, in its stead." In fact more than a quarter of it (corresponding roughly to pp. 18–25 of this reprint) is substantially, and for the most part verbally, identical with the conclusion of the substituted piece.[1] Many of the verbal variations are such as cannot be readily recorded in an *apparatus criticus*; but attention is called to some readings, and especially to the italics of the manuscript, which in the print of 1818 may have been suppressed beyond the author's intention.

The manuscript consists of a single gathering of sixteen unnumbered leaves measuring $6 \times 3\frac{5}{8}$ inches. The watermark is dated 1812. At the top of the first leaf is written *July 8*. At the foot of 14^r is written *Finis. July 16. 1816.* This is erased, and on the verso is added the last paragraph of

[1] See pp. 283–292 of the last volume of the edition of 1818.

PREFACE

the book; at the foot is *Finis. July 18. 1816*. The fifteenth and sixteenth leaves contain a passage belonging to the cancelled chapter (but not itself cancelled; see the notes to pages 22-25).

On the last leaf is pasted a strip of paper on which is written in pencil (possibly in Jane Austen's hand) and written over in ink (in another hand) *The Contents of this Drawer for Anna*—i. e. her niece Anna Lefroy.

This precious fragment has recently found its last home in the British Museum.

PERSUASION

Chapters 10 and 11 of the
Second Volume
as first planned

CHAP. 10

July 8.

With all this knowledge of M^r E—& this authority to impart it, Anne left Westgate Build^{gs}—her mind deeply busy in revolving what she had heard, feeling, thinking, recalling & forseeing everything; shocked at Mr Elliot—sighing over future Kellynch, and pained for Lady Russell, whose confidence in him had been entire.—The Embarrassment which must be felt from this hour in his presence!—How to behave to him?—how to get rid of him? —what to do by any of the Party at home?—where to be blind? where to be active?—It was altogether a confusion

fusion of Images & Doubts—a perplexity, an agitation which she could not see the end of—and she was in Gay Sᵗ & still so much engrossed, that she started on being addressed by Admˡ Croft, as if he were a person unlikely to be met there. It was within a few steps of his own door.—
" You are going to call upon my wife, said he, she will be very glad to see you."—Anne denied it " No—she really had not time, she was in her way home "—but while she spoke, the Admˡ had stepped back & knocked at the door, calling out, " Yes, yes, do go in; she is all alone. go in & rest yourself."—Anne felt so little disposed at this time to be in company of any sort, that it vexed her to be thus constrained—but she was obliged to stop.
" Since you are so very kind, said she, I will just ask Mʳˢ Croft how she does,
but

but I really cannot stay 5 minutes.—
You are sure she is quite alone."—The
possibility of Capt. W. had occurred
—and most fearfully anxious was she
to be assured—either that he was
within or that he was not; *which*,
might have been a question.—" Oh !
yes, quite alone—Nobody but her
Mantuamaker with her, & they have
been shut up together this half hour,
so it must be over soon."—" Her
Mantua maker !—then I am sure my
calling now, w^d be most inconvenient.—
Indeed you must allow me to leave my
Card & be so good as to explain it
afterwards to Mrs C." " No, no, not at
all, not at all. She will be very happy
to see you. Mind—I will not swear
that she has not something particular
to say to you—but *that* will all come
out in the right place. I give no hints.
—Why, Miss Elliot, we begin to hear
strange

strange things of you—(smiling in her face)—But you have not much the Look of it—as Grave as a little Judge."—Anne blushed.—"Aye, aye, that will do. Now, it is right. I *thought* we were not mistaken." She was left to guess at the direction of his Suspicions ;—the first wild idea had been of some disclosure from his B^r in law—but she was ashamed the next moment—& felt how far more probable that he should be meaning Mr E.—The door was opened—& the Man evidently beginning to *deny* his Mistress, when the sight of his Master stopped him. The Adm^l enjoyed the joke exceedingly. Anne thought his triumph over Stephen rather too long. At last however, he was able to invite her upstairs, & stepping before her said—" I will just go up with you myself & shew you in—. I cannot stay, because I must go to the
P. Office

P. Office, but if you will only sit down for 5 minutes I am sure Sophy will come—and you will find nobody to disturb you—there is nobody but Frederick here—" opening the door as he spoke.—Such a person to be passed over as a Nobody to *her* !—After being allowed to feel quite secure—indifferent—at her ease, to have it burst on her that she was to be the next moment in the same room with him !—No time for recollection !—for planning behaviour, or regulating manners !—There was time only to turn pale, before she had passed through the door, & met the astonished eyes of Capt. W—. who was sitting by the fire pretending to read & prepared for no greater surprise than the Admiral's hasty return.— Equally unexpected was the meeting, on each side. There was nothing to be done however, but to stifle feelings &
be

be quietly polite;—and the Admiral was too much on the alert, to leave any troublesome pause.—He repeated again what he had said before about his wife & everybody—insisted on Anne's sitting down & being perfectly comfortable, was sorry he must leave her himself, but was sure Mrs Croft w^d be down very soon, & w^d go upstairs & give her notice directly.—Anne *was* sitting down, but now she arose again—to entreat him not to interrupt M^rs C— & re-urge the wish of going away & calling another time.—But the Adm^l would not hear of it;—and if she did not return to the charge with unconquerable Perseverance, or did not with a more passive Determination walk quietly out of the room—(as certainly she might have done) may she not be pardoned?—If she *had* no horror of a few minutes Tète a Tète with Capt. W—, may she not be pardoned

pardoned for not wishing to give him the idea that she *had* ?—She reseated herself, & the Adm¹ took leave; but on reaching the door, said, " Frederick, a word with *you*, if you please."—Capt. W— went to him; and instantly, before they were well out of the room, the Adm¹ continued—" As I am going to leave you together, it is but fair I should give you something to talk of— & so, if you please—" Here the door was very firmly closed; she could guess by which of the two; and she lost entirely what immediately followed; but it was impossible for her not to distinguish parts of the rest, for the Adm¹ on the strength of the Door's being shut was speaking without any management of voice, tho' she c^d hear his companion trying to check him.— She could not doubt their being speaking of her. She heard her own name
&

& *Kellynch* repeatedly—she was very much distressed. She knew not what to do, or what to expect—and among other agonies felt the possibility of Capt. W—'s not returning into the room at all, which after *her* consenting to stay would have been—too bad for Language.—They seemed to be talking of the Adm^{ls} Lease of Kellynch. She heard him say something of " the Lease being signed or not signed "—*that* was not likely to be a very agitating subject—but then followed " I hate to be at an uncertainty—I must know at once—Sophy thinks the same." Then, in a lower tone, Capt. W— seemed remonstrating—wanting to be excused —wanting to put something off. "Phoo, Phoo—answered the Admiral now is the Time. If *you* will not speak, I will stop & speak myself."—" Very well Sir, very well Sir, followed with some impatience

impatience from his companion, opening the door as he spoke.—" You will then—you promise you will ? " replied the Admiral, in all the power of his natural voice, unbroken even by one thin door.—" Yes—Sir—Yes." And the Adm¹ was hastily left, the door was closed, and the moment arrived in which Anne was alone with Capt. W—. She could not attempt to see how he looked; but he walked immediately to a window, as if irresolute & embarrassed;—and for about the space of 5 seconds, she repented what she had done—censured it as unwise, blushed over it as indelicate.—She longed to be able to speak of the weather or the Concert—but could only compass the releif of taking a Newspaper in her hand.—The distressing pause was soon over however; he turned round in half a minute, and coming towards the Table where

where she sat, said, in a voice of effort & constraint—"You must have heard too much already Madam to be in any doubt of my having promised Adm¹ Croft to speak to you on some particular subject—& this conviction determines me to do it—however repugnant to my—to all my sense of propriety, to be taking so great a liberty.— You will acquit me of Impertinence I trust, by considering me as speaking only for another, and speaking by Necessity;—and the Adm¹ is a Man who can never be thought Impertinent by one who knows him as you do—. His Intentions are always the kindest & the Best;—and you will perceive that he is actuated by none other, in the application which I am now with— with very peculiar feelings—obliged to make."—He stopped—but merely to recover breath;—not seeming to expect
any

any answer.—Anne listened, as if her Life depended on the issue of his Speech.—He proceeded, with a forced alacrity.—" The Adm¹, Madam, was this morning confidently informed that you were—upon my word I am quite at a loss, ashamed—(breathing & speaking quick)—the awkwardness of *giving* Information of this sort to one of the Parties—You can be at no loss to understand me—It was very confidently said that Mʳ Elliot—that everything was settled in the family for an Union between Mʳ Elliot—& yourself. It was added that you were to live at Kellynch —that Kellynch was to be given up. This, the Admiral knew could not be correct—But it occurred to him that it might be the *wish* of the Parties— And my commission from him Madam, is to say, that if the Family wish is such, his Lease of Kellynch shall be
cancel'd

cancel'd, & he & my sister will provide themselves with another home, without imagining themselves to be doing anything which under similar circumstances w^d not be done for *them*.—This is all Madam.—A very few words in reply from you will be sufficient.— That *I* should be the person commissioned on this subject is extraordinary! —and beleive me Madam, it is no less painful.—A very few words however will put an end to the awkwardness & distress we may *both* be feeling." Anne spoke a word or two, but they were un-intelligible—And before she could command herself, he added,— " If you only tell me that the Adm^l may address a Line to Sir Walter, it will be enough. Pronounce only the words, *he may*.—I shall immediately follow him with your message.—" This was spoken, as with a fortitude which
seemed

seemed to meet the message.—" No Sir—said Anne—There is no message. —You are misin—the Adm¹ is misinformed.—I do justice to the kindness of his Intentions, but he is quite mistaken. There is no Truth in any such report."—He was a moment silent.—She turned her eyes towards him for the first time since his re-entering the room. His colour was varying—& he was looking at her with all the Power & Keenness, which she beleived no other eyes than his, possessed. "*No* Truth in any such report! —he repeated.—No Truth in any *part* of it?"—"None."—He had been standing by a chair—enjoying the releif of leaning on it—or of playing with it;—he now sat down—drew it a little nearer to her—& looked, with an expression which had something more than penetration in it, something softer

softer;—Her Countenance did not discourage.—It was a silent, but a very powerful Dialogue;—on his side, Supplication, on her's acceptance.—Still, a little nearer—and a hand taken and pressed—and " Anne, my own dear Anne ! "—bursting forth in the fullness of exquisite feeling—and all Suspense & Indecision were over.—They were re-united. They were restored to all that had been lost. They were carried back to the past, with only an increase of attachment & confidence, & only such a flutter of present Delight as made them little fit for the interruption of M*rs* Croft, when she joined them not long afterwards.—*She* probably, in the observations of the next ten minutes, saw something to suspect—& tho' it was hardly possible for a woman of her description to wish the Mantuamaker had imprisoned her longer, she might be

very

very likely wishing for some excuse to run about the house, some storm to break the windows above, or a summons to the Admiral's Shoemaker below.—Fortune favoured them all however in another way—in a gentle, steady rain—just happily set in as the Admiral returned & Anne rose to go.— She was earnestly invited to stay dinner;—a note was dispatched to Camden Place—and she staid;—staid till 10 at night. And during that time, the Husband & wife, either by the wife's contrivance, or by simply going on in their usual way, were frequently out of the room together—gone up stairs to hear a noise, or down stairs to settle their accounts, or upon the Landing place to trim the Lamp.— And these precious moments were turned to so good an account that all the most anxious feelings of the past were

were gone through.—Before they parted at night, Anne had the felicity of being assured in the first place that —(so far from being altered for the worse!)—she had *gained* inexpressibly in personal Loveliness; & that as to Character—her's was now fixed on his Mind as Perfection itself—maintaining the just Medium of Fortitude & Gentleness;—that he had never ceased to love & prefer her, though it had been only at Uppercross that he had learn't to do her Justice—& only at Lyme that he had begun to understand his own sensations;—that at Lyme he had received Lessons of more than one kind;—the passing admiration of Mr Elliot had at least *roused* him, and the scenes on the Cobb & at Capt. Harville's had fixed her superiority.— In his preceding *attempts* to attach himself to Louisa Musgrove, (the attempts

tempts of Anger & Pique)—he protested that he had continually felt the impossibility of really caring for Louisa, though till *that day*, till the leisure for reflection which followed it, he had not understood the perfect excellence of the Mind, with which Louisa's could so ill bear a comparison, or the perfect, the unrivalled hold it possessed over his own.—There he had learnt to distinguish between the steadiness of Principle & the Obstinacy of Self-will, between the Darings of Heedlessness, & the Resolution of a collected Mind— there he had seen everything to exalt in his estimation the Woman he had lost, & there begun to deplore the pride, the folly, the madness of resentment which had kept him from trying to regain her, when thrown in his way. From that period to the present had his penance been the most severe.—He had no
sooner

sooner been free from the horror & remorse attending the first few days of Louisa's accident, no sooner begun to feel himself alive again, than he had begun to feel himself though alive, not at liberty.—He found that he was considered by his friend Harville, as an engaged Man. The Harvilles entertained not a doubt of a mutual attachment between him & Louisa—and though this to *a degree*, was contradicted instantly—it yet made him feel that perhaps by *her* family, by everybody, by *herself* even, the same idea might be held—and that he was not *free* in honour—though, if such were to be the conclusion, too free alas! in Heart.—He had never thought justly on this subject before—he had not sufficiently considered that his excessive Intimacy at Uppercross must have it's danger of ill consequence in many

many ways, and that while trying whether he c^d attach himself to either of the Girls, he might be exciting unpleasant reports, if not, raising unrequited regard!—He found, too late, that he had entangled himself—and that precisely as he became thoroughly satisfied of his not *caring* for Louisa at all, he must regard himself as bound to her, if her feelings for him, were what the Harvilles supposed.—It determined him to leave Lyme—& await her perfect recovery elsewhere. He would gladly weaken, by any *fair* means, whatever sentiments or speculations concerning him might exist; and he went therefore into Shropshire meaning after a while, to return to the Crofts at Kellynch, & act as he found requisite.— He had remained in Shropshire, lamenting the Blindness of his own Pride, & the Blunders of his own Calculations, till

till at once released from Louisa by the astonishing felicity of her engagement with Benwicke. Bath, Bath—had instantly followed, in *Thought*; & not long after, in *fact*. To Bath, to arrive with Hope, to be torn by Jealousy at the first sight of M^r E—, to experience all the changes of each at the Concert, to be miserable by this morning's circumstantial report, to be now, more happy than Language could express, or any heart but his own be capable of.

He was very eager & very delightful in the description of what he had felt at the Concert.—The Even^g seemed to have been made up of exquisite moments;—the moment of her stepping forward in the Octagon Room to speak to him—the moment of M^r E's appearing & tearing her away, & one or two subsequent moments, marked by returning hope, or increasing Despondence

dence, were all dwelt on with energy. " To see you, cried he, in the midst of those who could not be *my* well-wishers, to see your Cousin close by you—conversing & smiling—& feel all the horrible Eligibilities & Proprieties of the Match!—to consider it as the certain wish of every being who could hope to influence you—even, if your own feelings were reluctant, or indifferent—to consider what powerful supports would be his!—Was not it enough to make the fool of me, which my behaviour expressed?—How could I look on without agony?—Was not the very sight of the *Friend* who sat behind you?—was not the recollection of what *had* been—the knowledge of her Influence—the indelible, immoveable Impression of what *Persuasion* had *once* done, was not it all against me?"—

" You should have distinguished—replied

plied Anne—You should not have suspected me *now*;—The case so different, & my age so different!—If I *was* wrong, in yeilding to Persuasion once, remember that it was to Persuasion exerted on the side of Safety, not of Risk. When I yeilded, I thought it was to *Duty*.—But no *Duty* could be called in aid here.—In marrying a Man indifferent to me, all Risk would have been incurred, & all Duty violated."—
" Perhaps I ought to have reasoned thus, he replied, but I could not.—I could not derive benefit from the later knowledge of your Character which I had acquired, I could not bring it into play, it was overwhelmed, buried, lost in those earlier feelings, which I had been smarting under Year after Year.— I could think of you only as one who *had* yeilded, who *had* given me up, who *had* been influenced by any one rather than

than by *me*—I saw you with the very Person who had guided you in that year of Misery—I had no reason to think her of less authority now;—the force of Habit was to be added."—" I should have thought, said Anne, that my Manner to yourself, might have spared you much, or all of this."— " No—No—Your manner might be only the ease, which your engagement to another Man would give.—I left you with this beleif.—And yet—I was determined to see you again.—My spirits rallied with the morning, & I felt that I had still a motive for remaining here.—The Admirals news indeed, was a revulsion. Since that moment, I have been decided what to do—and had it been confirmed, this would have been my *last day* in Bath."

There was time for all this to pass— with such Interruptions only as enhanced

hanced the charm of the communication—and Bath c^d scarcely contain any other two Beings at once so rationally & so rapturously happy as during that even^g occupied the Sopha of Mrs Croft's Drawing room in Gay S^t.

Capt. W.— had taken care to meet the Adm^l as he returned into the house, to satisfy him as to M^r E— & Kellynch;—and the delicacy of the Admiral's good nature kept him from saying another word on the subject to Anne.—He was quite concerned lest he might have been giving her pain by touching a tender part. Who could say?—She might be liking her Cousin, better than he liked her.—And indeed, upon recollection, if they had been to marry at all why should they have waited so long?—

When the Even^g closed, it is probable that the Adm^l received some new Ideas from

from his Wife;—whose particularly friendly manner in parting with her, gave Anne the gratifying persuasion of her seeing & approving.

It had been such a day to Anne!—the hours which had passed since her leaving Camden Place, had done so much!—She was almost bewildered, almost too happy in looking back.—It was necessary to sit up half the Night & lie awake the remainder to comprehend with composure her present state, & pay for the overplus of Bliss, by Headake & Fatigue.—

CHAPTER

CHAPTER 11.

Who can be in doubt of what followed?—When any two Young People take it into their heads to marry, they are pretty sure by perseverance to carry their point—be they ever so poor, or ever so imprudent, or ever so little likely to be necessary to each other's ultimate comfort. This may be bad Morality to conclude with, but I beleive it to be Truth—and if such parties succeed, how should a Capt. W— & an Anne E—, with the advantage of maturity of Mind, consciousness of Right, & one Independant Fortune between them, fail of bearing down every opposition? They might in fact, have born down a great deal
more

more than they met with, for there was little to distress them beyond the want of Graciousness & Warmth. Sir W. made no objection, & Eliz^{th} did nothing worse than look cold & unconcerned.—Capt. W— with £25,000— & as high in his Profession as Merit & Activity c^d place him, was no longer nobody. He was now esteemed quite worthy to address the Daughter of a foolish spendthrift Baronet, who had not had Principle or sense enough to maintain himself in the Situation in which Providence had placed him, & who c^d give his Daughter but a small part of the share of ten Thousand pounds which must be her's hereafter. —Sir Walter indeed tho' he had no affection for his Daughter & no vanity flattered to make him really happy on the occasion, was very far from thinking it a bad match for her.—On the contrary

contrary when he saw more of Capt. W.— & eyed him well, he was very much struck by his personal claims & felt that *his* superiority of appearance might be not unfairly balanced against *her* superiority of Rank;—and all this, together with his well-sounding name, enabled Sir W. at last to prepare his pen with a very good grace for the insertion of the Marriage in the volume of Honour.—The only person among them whose opposition of feelings c^d excite any serious anxiety, was Lady Russel. —Anne knew that Lady R— must be suffering some pain in understanding & relinquishing M^r E— & be making some struggles to become truly acquainted with & do justice to Capt. W.—This however, was what Lady R— had now to do. She must learn to feel that she had been mistaken with regard to both—that she had been
unfairly

unfairly influenced by appearances in each—that, because Capt. W.'s manners had not suited her own ideas, she had been too quick in suspecting them to indicate a Character of dangerous Impetuosity, & that because Mʳ Elliot's manners had precisely pleased her in their propriety & correctness, their general politeness & suavity, she had been too quick in receiving them as the certain result of the most correct opinions & well regulated Mind.— There was nothing less for Lady R. to do than to admit that she had been pretty completely wrong, & to take up a new set of opinions & hopes.— There *is* a quickness of perception in some, a nicety in the discernment of character—a natural Penetration in short which no Experience in others can equal—and Lady R. had been less gifted in this part of Understanding than

than her young friend;—but she was a very good Woman; & if her second object was to be sensible & well judging, her first was to see Anne happy. She loved Anne better than she loved her own abilities—and when the awkwardness of the Beginning was over, found little hardship in attaching herself as a Mother to the Man who was securing the happiness of her Child. Of all the family, Mary was probably the one most immediately gratified by the circumstance. It was creditable to have a Sister married, and she might flatter herself that she had been greatly instrumental to the connection, by having Anne staying with her in the Autumn; & as her own Sister must be better than her Husbands Sisters, it was very agreable that Captn W— should be a richer Man than either Capt. B. or Charles Hayter.—She had

something to suffer perhaps when they came into contact again, in seeing Anne restored to the rights of Seniority & the Mistress of a very pretty Landaulet— but *she* had a *future* to look forward to, of powerful consolation—Anne had no Uppercross Hall before her, no Landed Estate, no Headship of a family, and if they could but keep Capt. W— from being made a Baronet, she would not change situations with Anne.—It would be well for the *Eldest* Sister if she were equally satisfied with *her* situation, for a change is not very probable there. —She had soon the mortification of seeing Mr E. withdraw, & no one of proper condition has since presented himself to raise even the unfounded hopes which sunk with *him*. The news of his Cousin Anne's engagement burst on Mr Elliot most unexpectedly. It deranged his best plan of domestic
Happiness

Happiness, his best hopes of keeping Sir Walter single by the watchfulness which a son in law's rights w^d have given—But tho' discomfited & disappointed, he c^d still do something for his own interest & his own enjoyment. He soon quitted Bath and on Mrs Clay's quitting it likewise soon afterwards & being next heard of, as established under his Protection in London, it was evident how double a Game he had been playing, & how determined he was to save himself from being cut out by *one* artful woman at least.— Mrs Clay's affections had overpowered her Interest, & she had sacrificed for the Young Man's sake, the possibility of scheming longer for Sir Walter ;— she has Abilities however as well as Affections, and it is now a doubtful point whether his cunning or hers may finally carry the day, whether, after
preventing

preventing her from being the wife of Sir Walter, he may not be wheedled & caressed at last into making her the wife of Sir William.—

It cannot be doubted that Sir Walter & Eliz: were shocked & mortified by the loss of their companion & the discovery of their deception in her. They had their great cousins to be sure, to resort to for comfort—but they must long feel that to flatter & follow others, without being flattered & followed themselves is but a state of half enjoyment.

Anne, satisfied at a very early period, of Lady Russel's *meaning* to love Capt. W— as she ought, had no other alloy to the happiness of her prospects, than what arose from the consciousness of having no relations to bestow on him which a Man of Sense could value. —There, she felt her own Inferiority keenly.—The disproportion in their fortunes

fortunes was nothing ;—it did not give her a moment's regret ;—but to have no Family to receive & estimate him properly, nothing of respectability, of Harmony, of Goodwill to offer in return for all the Worth & all the prompt welcome which met her in his Brothers & Sisters, was a source of as lively pain, as her Mind could well be sensible of, under circumstances of otherwise strong felicity.—She had but two friends in the World, to add to his List, Lady R. & Mrs Smith.—To those however, he was very well-disposed to attach himself. Lady R— inspite of all her former transgressions, he could now value from his heart ;—while he was not obliged to say that he beleived her to have been right in originally dividing them, he was ready to say almost anything else in her favour ;—& as for Mrs Smith, she had claims of various kinds

kinds to recommend her quickly & permanently.—Her recent good offices by Anne had been enough in themselves—and their marriage, instead of depriving her of one friend secured her two. She was one of their first visitors in their settled Life—and Capt. Wentworth, by putting her in the way of recovering her Husband's property in the W. Indies, by writing for her, & acting for her, & seeing her through all the petty Difficulties of the case, with the activity & exertion of a fearless Man, & a determined friend, fully requited the services she had rendered, or had ever meant to render, to his Wife. Mrs Smith's enjoyments were not *spoiled* by this improvement of Income, with some improvement of health, & the acquisition of such friends to be often with, for her chearfulness & mental Activity did not fail her, & while

while those prime supplies of Good remained, she might have bid defiance even to greater accessions of worldly Prosperity. She might have been absolutely rich & perfectly healthy, & yet be happy.—*Her* spring of Felicity was in the glow of her Spirits—as her friend Anne's was in the warmth of her Heart.—Anne was Tenderness itself ;— and she had the full worth of it in Captn Wentworth's affection. His Profession was all that could ever make her friends wish *that* Tenderness less; the dread of a future War, all that could dim her Sunshine.—She gloried in being a Sailor's wife, but she must pay the tax of quick alarm, for belonging to that Profession which is—if possible—more distinguished in it's Domestic Virtues, than in it's National Importance.—

FINIS

July 18.—1816.

Chap. 10.   July 8

With all this knowledge of Mr. E.
& sister ^[authority] her ^[after] ~~confirmation~~ of it
Anne ~~quitted~~ ^[left] Westgate Build.s — her
mind deeply busy in revolving what she
had heard, feeling, thinking, recalling
& foreseeing every thing, shocked at ~~what~~
~~she felt~~; ^[better & worse,] sighing over ^[the] future. & though
pained for Lady Russell's ~~I supp~~ ^[glancing at the]
~~complacency~~ ~~complacency & considering how~~
~~her~~ ~~confidence~~ ^[how entire her]
~~had been entire.~~ ~~&~~ The Embarass-
ment which must be felt from this
~~moment~~ ^[hour] in his presence — How to behave to him, — how to get rid of him.
What to do by any of the Party at
home, — where to be believed, where
to be active — It was altogether a
confusion of Images & Doubts — a
perplexity, an ^[agitating] ~~uneasiness~~, which
she could not see the end of. —
And She was in Gay St. & still so
~~quite~~ engrossed, ~~she~~ ^[that she started] at being
addressed by Adm.l Croft, as if ^[a]
person unlikely to be met there.

It was within a few steps of his
own door.— "You are going to call
upon my sister, said he, she will
be very glad to see you—" Anne
said "No – she really had not time,
she was in her way home." but
while she spoke, the Adml had stept
back. "I know you will, all at once, calling out her
"Yes, yes, do go in; go & see & wish
yourself." Anne felt so little disposed at this time to be in any
company of any sort, that just
of whatever description, that she was
really unwilling to be thus constrained –
but she was now obliged to stop.
"Since you are very so kind, said
she, I will just ask Mrs Croft.
"how she does, but I really cannot
stay 5 minutes." "Oh, yes you are sure.
she is quite alone. and oh! ah!
be had insured, and once –
at once for fully answered to have
refused. either that he was & this
or that he was not – he could not
have been without hearing – "oh yes,
quite alone – Nobody but her
Mlle Musgrove with her, & they
have been shut up together these
half hour, so it must be over
soon."

"The Mantuamaker! — then I am sure my calling now wᵈ. be most inconvenient. — Indeed you must allow me ~~very good as to~~ to leave me & lead ~~or explain it~~ afterwards to Miss —"

"No, no, not at all, not at all, if she will be ~~very happy to~~ see you; I will not swear that she has not something particular to say to you, but that will all come out in the right place. — I give no hints; — why, Miss Elliot, we begin to hear strange things of you, (smiling in her face) — But ~~I do not~~ ~~scarcely one~~ much in look of ~~little sister~~ ~~for I am sure~~ ~~sir, ever so little a~~ ~~her~~ ~~more~~ blushed. — Aye, aye, that will do. Now, it is all right. I thought we were not mistaken."

~~She~~ was left to guess at the direction of his suspicions; — the ~~first idea~~ had been of some ~~information after~~ ~~from his B~~ ~~ ~~ ~~ — but she was ashamed the next moment ~~ ~~ ~~ felt that~~ how far ~~more probable. ~~ ~~it was that he shaped~~ ~~~~ the meaning Mʳ. E. — The door was opened — & the Man ~~was~~ evidently beginning to deny his Mistress, when the sight of his Master stopped him. The Admᵈ. enjoyed

the joke exceedingly. Anne thought he
triumphs over Stephen rather too long.
At last however, he was able to in=
=vite her upstairs & stepping before her
said — "I will just go up with
you myself & shew you in — I cannot
stay, because I must go to the P. Office,
but if you will only sit down for
5 minutes I am sure Sophy will
come. — And you will find nobody
to disturb you — there is nobody but
Frederick here." — opening the door as
he spoke. — Such a person to be passed
over as a Nobody to her! — After being
allowed to feel quite secure — indifferent
— at her ease, to have it burst on her
that she was to be the next moment
in the same room with him! —
No time for recollection! — for plan:
:ning behaviour, or regulating man:
:ners! — There was time only to turn
pale, before she had passed through the
door, & met the astonished eyes of
Capt. Wentworth, who was sitting by the
fire, pretending to read & prepared for
no greater surprise than the Admiral's
hasty return. — Equally unexpected
was the meeting, on each side. There
was nothing to be done however but
to stifle feelings & be quietly polite; —
and the Admiral was too much on the

that, to leave them any troublesome
hanger. — He repeated again what he had
said before ~~about his wife & everybody~~
~~give his wife notice~~ insisted on Anne's
sitting down & being perfectly comfortable —
was sorry he must leave her himself,
but was sure W^m & Croft w^d. be down
very soon, & w^d. go up stairs & give
her notice directly. — Anne ~~was~~ sitting
down, but now she arose again
to entreat him not to interrupt M^{rs} C.
& renew the wish of going away or
calling another time. But there ~~Adm~~.
could not hear of it; and if she did
not return to the charge ~~with~~ unconquerable Perseverance, ~~with determined~~
~~passive Determination~~ or with a more
~~think~~ & walk quietly out of the room
— (as certainly she might & have done)
may she not be pardoned? — If she
had no horror of a few minutes
Tête à Tête with Capt. W^m, may
she not be pardoned for not
waiting to give him the idea that
she had. ~~?~~ She seated herself, &
the Adm^l. took leave; "Frederick, a
word with you, if you please."
~~Frederick turned down Capt. W — present~~
~~being ~~ and they did go together~~ ~~a few~~
~~giving out of the room — ~~ ~~he looks~~
~~were nothing did speak — indeed~~ ~~so~~
~~than leave them together it is ~~~~i~~
but having

I should give you something to
talk of & so, if you please."—
Here the door was very firmly closed;
she could guess by which of the two;
and she lost entirely what immedi-
-ately followed. Probably it was impossible
for her not to distinguish parts of the rest,
but the Adml. on the strength of the
Don's being sleaf, was she being without
any management of voice, tho' she cd. hear
his companion trying in vain to under take
to check him.— She could not doubt
their being speaking of her. She heard
her own name & Kellynch repeatedly—
She was very much distressed. She knew
not what to do, or what to expect, & possibly
and among other agonies felt the same
of Capt. W—'s not returning into the
room at all; which after her consenting to
stay would have been.— too bad
for language.— They seemed to be
talking of the Adml's Lease of Kellynch
she heard him say something of the Lease being
signed or not signed — that was not likely to be
a very agitating subject.— "I hate to
be at an uncertainty— I must know
at once— Sophy thinks the same."
Then in a lower tone, Capt. W.—
wanting to be cleared, or wanting to put something
Seemed remonstrating, wanting to have explained
Now, then, enquired why not ask her
now is the time. If you will not—

speak. I will speak myself... "very well Sir, very well Sir," with some impatience, followed from his companion, opening the door as he spoke. "I will then — you promise you will" — replied the Admiral, — "all the importance of his signal voice unbroken even by one their door, hastily "Yes Sir, yes." And the Adm¹. was left; & the door was closed, and the moment arrived in which Anne was alone with Capt. W——. She could not attempt to see how he looked; but he walked immediately to a window, as if irresolute & embarrassed; — for about the space of 5 seconds, she repeated what she had done — censured it as unwise, blushed over it as indelicate — She longed to be able to speak of the weather or the Concert — but could only compass the relief of taking a Newspaper in her hand. — The distressing pause was soon over however; he turned round in half a minute, & coming towards the table, as if he sat said, in a voice of effort & constraint, "You must have heard too much — Madam, already, doubt of my having promised the Admirl. Crofts to speak to you on some particular subject — & this conviction determines me to do it — however repugnant to my feelings — to all my sense of propriety, to be taking so great a Liberty! — You will acquit me of Impertinence I trust, by considering me as speaking only for another, & speaking by Necessity; — and the Adml. is a Man who can never be thought Impertinent by one who knows him as you do. His Intentions are always the kindest & the best; — & you will perceive that he is actuated by none other, in the application which I am now with — with very peculiar feelings — obliged to make." — He stopped — but merely to recover breath; — not seeming to expect any answer. — Anne listened, as if her Life depended on the issue of his Speech. — He proceeded, with a forced alacrity. "The Admiral, Madam, was this morning confidently informed that you were — (upon my word, I am quite at a Loss, really ashamed — (breathing & speaking quick) — that awkwardness of giving Information of this sort to one of the Parties — You can be at no loss to understand me — It was very confidently said that Mr Elliot — that everything was settled in the family for an Union between Mr Elliot & Yourself. — It was added that you were to live at Kellynch — that Kellynch was to be given up. This, the Admiral could not but, of course, but it occurred to him that it might be the wish of the Parties. And my commission from Madam, is to say, that if the family-wish is such, his Lease of Kellynch shall be cancell'd, & he & my Sister will provide themselves with another home, without imagining themselves to be doing anything which under similar circumstances would not be done for them. — This is all, Madam. — A very few words in reply from you will be sufficient. — That I should be the person commissioned on this subject, is extraordinary! and believe me, Madam, it is no less painful. — A very few words however will put an end to the awkwardness & distress we may both be feeling."

Anne spoke a word or two, but they were not intelligible. — And be-
fore she could command herself, he added. "If you only tell me that the Adml. may address a line to Sir —, it will be enough. I shall immediately follow him with your message." — This was spoken, as with as Gratitude which seemed to mark the message. "No Sir — said Anne. There is no message. — You are mis-in— — the Adml. is misinformed. — I do justice to the kindness of his Intentions, but he is quite mistaken. There is no truth in any such report." — He was a moment silent. — She turned her eyes towards him for the first time since his re-entering the room. His colour was receding — & his eyes looking at her with all the power & keenness, which she believed no other eyes than his, possessed. — "No truth in any such report! — he repeated. — No truth in any part of it?" "None." — He had been standing by a chair — enjoying the relief of leaning on it, or of playing with it; — he now sat down — drew it a little nearer to her — & looked, with an expression which had something more than penetration in it, something softer. — His Countenance did not

discourage. It was a silent, but a very powerful Dialogue;—on his side, Suppli=cation, on her's acceptance.—Still, a little nearer—and a hand taken and pressed—and "Anne, my own dear Anne!"—bursting forth in the fullness of exquisite feeling—and all suspense & Indecision were over.—They were re-united. They were restored to all that had been lost. They were carried back to the past, with only an increase of attachment & confidence, & only such a flutter of present Delight as made them little fit for the interruption of Mrs Croft, when she joined them not long afterwards.— She probably, in the observations of the next ten minutes, saw something to suspect—& tho' it was hardly possible for a Woman of her description to wish the Mantuamaker had imprisoned her longer, she might very likely be wishing for some excuse to run about the house, some storm to break the windows above, or a summons to the Admiral's Shoemaker below.—Fortune favoured them all however in another way—in a gentle, steady rain—just happily set in as the Admiral returned.

& Anne rose to go. — She was earnestly invited to stay dinner; — a
note was dispatched to Camden Place, and
she staid; — staid till 10 at night.
And during that time, ~~scarcely an~~
~~interval was secured to the two by the~~
~~Crofts~~ the Husband & wife, either by
the wife's contrivance, or by simply going
on in their usual way, were frequently
out of the room together — gone up
stairs to hear a noise, or ~~gone~~ down
stairs to settle their accounts, or
~~gone~~ upon the Landing place to trim
the Lamp. — And these precious moments
were turned to so good an account that
~~many~~ all of the most anxious feelings of the
past were gone through. — Before they
parted at night, Anne had the felicity
of being assured in the first place (so far from
being altered for the worse) — she
had gained inexpressibly in personal loveliness, &
that as to Character — his was now
fixed on her mind as Perfection it-
self — ~~having~~ maintaining the just Medium of
Fortitude & Gentleness — that he had
never ceased to love her, though it
had been — only at Uppercross that
he had learnt to do her ~~any~~ Jus-
-tice — & only at Lyme that he
had begun to understand his own
sensations; — that at Lyme he had

received lessons of more than one kind; the passing admiration of Mr Elliot had at least roused hers, and the scenes on the Cobb & at last Harvilles had fixed her superiority. In his succeeding attempts to attach himself to Louisa Musgrove, (the attempts of angry & pique,) he protested that he had continually felt the impossibility of really caring for her, though till that day, till the leisure for reflection which followed it, he had not understood the perfect excellence of the Mind, with which Louisa's could so ill bear a comparison, or the perfect, the unrivalled hold, it possessed over his own. — There he had learnt to distinguish between the steadiness of Principle & the Obstinacy of Self will, between the darings of Heedlessness, & the Resolution of a collected Mind. there he had seen everything to exalt in his estimation the Woman he had lost, & there begun to deplore the pride, the folly, the madness of resentment which had kept him from trying to regain her, when thrown in his way. From that period to the present

had his penance been the most
severe. — He had no sooner been
free from the horror & remorse
attending the first few days of
Louisa's accident, no sooner began
to feel himself alive again, than
he had begun to feel himself,
though alive, not at liberty. He
found that he was considered by his
friend Harville, as an engaged Man.
The Harvilles entertained not a doubt
of a mutual attachment between
him & Louisa — and though this
to a degree, was contradicted instantly —
it made him feel that perhaps by
her family, by every body, by him-
-self even, the same idea might be
held — and that he was not free
in honour — though, if such were
to be the conclusion, too fair, alas!
in Heart. He had never thought
justly on this subject before —
he had not sufficiently consi-
-dered that his excessive Intimacy
at Uppercross must have its danger
of ill consequence in many ways,
and that while trying whether
he c.d attach himself to either

of the Girls, he might be exciting unpleasant reports, if not, raising unrequited regard! — He found, too late, that he had entangled himself — and that precisely as he became thoroughly satisfied of his not caring for Louisa at all, he must regard himself as bound to her, if her feelings for him were what the Harvilles supposed. — It determined him to leave Lyme — & await her perfect recovery elsewhere. — He would gladly weaken, by any fair means, whatever sentiments or speculations concerning them might exist; and he went therefore into Shropshire, meaning after a while, to return to the Crofts at Kellynch, & act as he found requisite. — He had remained in Shropshire, lamenting the Blindness of his own Pride, the Blunders of his own Calculations, till at once released from Louisa by the astonishing felicity of her engagement with Benwick. — Bath, Bath — had instantly followed, in thought; & not long after, in fact. — To Bath, to arrive with Hopes, to be torn by Jealousy at the first reappearance of M^r E — , to expe=
:rience —

all the changes of such at the
onset, to be miserable by this
morning's circumstantial report, to
be now, more happy than Language
could express, on any heart but his
very own capable of. There was time
for all this to pass — With the
such Interceptions only as enhanced the charm of the communication
— and Bath ed. scarcely contain any
other two Beings at once rationally & so
rapturously happy as during that
evening occupied the Sopha of
Mrs Crofts Drawing room in Gay St.

Capt. W— had taken care to
meet the Adml as he returned into
the house, to satisfy him as to
Mr E. &
Kellynch;— and the delicacy
of the Admiral's good nature
kept him from saying another
word on the subject to Anne.
He was quite concerned lest he
might have been giving her
pain by touching a tender part.
Who could say? She might be
liking her Cousin better than
he liked her. And indeed,

upon recollection, if they had
been so many, all ~~it~~ ~~they should have done~~ ~~of the head.~~
~~tongue~~ ~~closed~~
When the door. ~~was~~
it is probable that the Adm.l
received some new ideas from his
wife; ~~the whole~~ particularly ~~find~~
~~manner in~~ ~~her~~ ~~of~~
with her, made Anne believe
~~she heard that~~ the gratifying
~~perception of his seeing~~ approving
~~what she saw or conjectured~~.

It had been such a day to
Anne! the hours which had
passed since her leaving Camden
Place, had done so much! —
She was almost bewildered, almost too happy in ~~reflecting~~
~~looking back~~. It was necessary to sit up
half the night & lie awake the
remainder, to comprehend with composure her present state, & pay
for the overplus of Bliss, by
headake & fatigue.

Chapter II.

Who can be in doubt of what followed? When any two young People take it into their heads to marry, they are pretty sure by perseverance to carry their point, be they ever so poor, or ever so imprudent, or ever so little likely to be necessary to each other's ultimate comfort. This may be bad Morality to conclude with, but I believe it to be Truth — and if such practice succeed, how should a Capt W. & an Anne W. fail, with the advantages of Maturity of Mind, consciousness of Right, & independent Fortune between them, of bearing down every opposition? They might in fact, have borne down a great deal more than they met with, for there was little to distress them beyond the want of Graciousness & Warmth. Sir W. made no objection, & Eliz: too: did nothing worse than look cold & unconcerned. — Capt. W. with £25,000 — & as high in his

Profession as Merit & activity could place him, was no longer nobody. He was now esteemed quite worthy to address the Daughter of a foolish spendthrift Baronet, who had not had principle or sense enough to maintain himself in the Situation in which Providence had placed him, & who could give his Daughter but a small part of the share of ten thousand pounds which must be hers hereafter. —Sir Walter indeed, tho' he had no affection for his daughter & no vanity flattered to make him really happy on the occasion, was very far from thinking it a bad match for her.—On the contrary when he saw more of Capt. W. saw him repeatedly by daylight & eyed him well, he was very much struck by his personal claims & felt that his superiority of appearance might be not unfairly balanced against her superiority of Rank; and all this, with his well-sounding name, enabled Sir W. at last to prepare his pen, with a very good grace for the insertion of the marriage in his handsome volume of Honour.—

prepared to be the best [struck] better acquaintance with themselves. — The only person among them, whose opposition of feelings c.d be at all excite anxiety on the subject, was Lady Russel. — Anne knew that Lady R — must be suffering some pain in understanding & relinquishing M.r E, — & be making some struggles to become truly acquainted with & do justice to Capt. W. — This however, was what Lady R. had now to do. She must learn to feel that she had been mistaken with regard to both — that she had been unfairly influenced by appearances in each. — That, because Capt W.'s manners had not suited her own ideas, she had been too quick in suspecting them to indicate a Character of dangerous Impetuousity; & that because M.r Elliot's manners had precisely pleased her in their propriety & correctness, their general politeness & suavity, she had been too quick in receiving them as the certain result of the most correct opinions & well-regulated

Mind. There was nothing for less
for Lady R. to do than to admit
that she had been pretty completely
wrong, & to take up a new set
of opinions & of hopes. ~~She had enough~~
~~quickness of perception, a nicety~~
~~again but now however having to~~
~~[illegible] in the discernment of character~~
~~a natural Penetration — in short [illegible]~~
~~[illegible] in others ca[illegible]~~
~~[illegible] any [illegible] [illegible] [illegible]~~
~~[illegible] Lady R. had been [illegible]~~
~~[illegible] of [illegible] I can [illegible]~~
~~gifted in [illegible] part of Understanding~~
~~[illegible] [illegible] [illegible] [illegible] [illegible] her friend~~
~~[illegible] to have given [illegible]~~
~~[illegible] [illegible] already appeared.~~
~~[illegible] [illegible] [illegible] point where~~
~~I thought myself [illegible] [illegible]~~
~~and shall leave it to the index~~
~~of [illegible] & Chapters & the in the~~
~~aged Ladies in general~~ — but she
was a very good woman; &
if her second object was to be sensible
& well judging, her first was to see
Anne happy. She loved Anne
better than she loved her own
abilities — and when the first
awkwardness of the Beginning was
over, found little hardship in
attaching herself ~~as a [illegible]~~

Mother to Charles Musgrove who she
was ~~certain~~ ~~~~ seeing
~~that~~ happiness of her ~~other~~ Child.
Of all the family, Mary was probably
the one most immediately gratified
~~~~ the circumstance. It was very
delightful to have a Sister married,
and she might flatter herself ~~that it had~~
~~been as her ~~~~ that ~~~~ had~~ the completion
been greatly instrumental to ~~~~ by
having Anne ~~staying~~ ~~~~ with her in
the Autumn; & as her own Sister
must be better than her Husband's
Sisters, it was very agreeable ~~~~
that Capt Wth should be a
richer Man than either Capt. B.
or Charles Hayter. — She had something to suffer perhaps, when
they came ~~~~ ~~together~~ again,
in seeing Anne restored to the
rights of Seniority & the Mistress
of a very pretty Landaulet. — but
she had a future to look forward
to, of powerful consolation — Anne
had no Uppercross Hall before her,
no Landed Estate, no Headship

of the Families, and if they could but keep Capt. W.— from being Knighted to make a Baronet. She would not change situations with some—. It would be well for the Eldest Sister if she were equally satisfied with her situation, — a change is not very probable, — she has, from the mortification of seeing Mr. E. withdraw, & no one of proper condition has since pre:=sented herself to raise even the unfounded hopes which sunk with him. The news of his Cousin Anne's engagement burst on Mr. Elliot most un=expectedly, unpleasantly. It derang'd his best plan of domestic Happiness, his best hopes of keeping Sir Walter single by the watchfulness which a Son in Law's rights w.d have given.— But tho' discomfited & disappointed, he'd still do something for his own Interest & his own Enjoyment.

He quitted Bath soon after, and
Miss Percy's ... soon after
& has never heard of, as establish-
under his Protection. ... London
... was ...
...
... & how
determined he was to save himself from being taken in by an
art'd woman at least. —
Miss Percy's affections had overpowered her Interest, & she had
sacrificed for the young Man's
sake, the power of Scheming
longer for Sir Walter; — she has
abilities however - as well as
Affections, and it is now a
doubtful point whether his ...
on her may finally ... ...
the day, ...
... Lady ... ...
Walter, after preventing her from
being the wife of Sir Walter, he
may not be ... & caused at last
making her the wife of Sir
William..

It cannot be doubted that Sir Walter & Eliz: were shocked & mortified by the loss of their companion & the discovery of their deception in to her. They had their great Cousins to be sure to resort to for comfort — but they must long feel that to flatter & follow others, without being flattered & followed themselves is but a state of half enjoyment.

Anne, satisfied at a very early period, of Lady Russel's meaning to love Capt. W— as she ought, had no other alloy to the happiness of her prospects, than what arose from the consciousness of having no relations to bestow on him which a Man of Sense could value. There she felt her own superiority keenly. The disproportion in their fortunes was nothing;—it did not give her a moment's regret; but to have no family to receive & estimate him properly, nothing of respectability, of harmony, of goodwill —

to offer in return for all the
worth & all the prompt welcome which met her in this Bro-
ther & Sister, was a source of
as keen pain, ~~to her~~ ~~feelings of~~ ~~upright Delicacy~~, as ^her feelings^ it could well
be sensible of under circumstances
of otherwise strong felicity. — She
had but two friends in the World
~~independent of herself, whose~~
~~ever~~ to add to ~~this list~~, Lady R.
& Mrs Smith. — ~~Lady R~~. To these
however, he was very well-disposed
to attach himself. Lady R — in
spite of all her former transgressions,
he could now value from this
period; — while he was not obliged
~~been~~ to say that he believed her to have
been ^originally^ in misleading them, he was
ready to say ^almost^ anything else in her
favour; — & as for Mrs Smith,
she had ~~equal~~ ~~unequal~~ claims of
various kinds to recommend her
quickly & permanently. — Her recent
good offices by Anne had been

enough in themselves — and their
means of being deprived of one,
friend by another in a manner, it
gained her another secured her two.
She was one of
their first visitors in their settled
Life — and Capt. Wentworth, by
putting her in the way of recovering her husband in the W. Indies,
by writing for her &
acting for her & seeing her through
all the petty Difficulties of the case
with the activity & exertion of a
fearless Man, & a determined
friend, convinced her of his
being much more Perfection
than even that with the
world had fully required. She
Services she had rendered or had ever
meant to render, to his
Wife

July 18.
1816.

Mrs Smith's enjoyments were but spoiled by this impediment of Income, with improvement of health, & the acquisition of such friends to be often with, for her cheerfulness & mental activity did not fail her, & while those prime supplies of Good remained, she might have bid defiance even to greater accessions of worldly Prosperity. She might have been absolutely rich & perfectly healthy, & yet be happy. — The spring of Felicity was in the glow of her Spirits — as her friend Anne's was in the warmth of her heart. — Anne was Tenderness itself; and she had all the full worth of it in Captain Wentworth's affection. His Profession was all that could ever make her friends wish that Tenderness less; the dread of a future War, all that could dim her Sunshine. — She gloried in being a Sailor's wife, but she must pay the tax of quick alarm, for belonging to that Profession which is, if possible, more distinguished in its Domestic Virtues, than in its National Importance.

Finis

July 18. 1816.

X
He was very eager & very delightful in the description of
what he had felt the week before—
the Evens. seemed to have been made
up of exquisite moments;—the
moment of her stepping forward in
the Octagon room, to speak to him;
the moment of Mr E.'s appearing
~~quietly~~ ~~instantly~~ ~~taking her
away~~, & one or two subsequent moments
~~towards~~, marked by returning hope,
or increasing ~~alarm~~ ~~despondence~~, were all
dwelt on with energy. ~~of Love~~
"To see you, ~~said~~ cried he, in the midst
of those who could not be my
well-wishers, to see your Cousin
close by you, ~~conversing~~ ~~smiling~~, to feel all the horrible
Eligibilities & Proprieties of the
Match!—to consider it as the
~~probable~~ certain wish of every being
who could hope to influence you
— even, if your own feelings were
reluctant, or indifferent—to
consider ~~that~~ what powerful
supports would be his!—Was

not it enough to make the fool
of, which my behaviour expressed?
— How could I look on without
feeling agony between danger? — was
not the very sight of the Friend
who sat behind you? was not
the recollection of what had been—
the knowledge of her Influence—
the indelible, immoveable Impression of
what Persuasion had once
done, was not it all against me!"—
"You should have distinguished—
replied Anne — you should not have
suspected me now; — The case is so
different, & my age so different.
If I was wrong, in yielding to
Persuasion once, remember that
it was to Persuasion exerted on
the side of Safety, not of Risk.
When I yielded, I thought it was
to Duty. But no Duty could
be called in aid here. In marrying
a Man indifferent to me, all
Risk would have been incurred,
& all Duty violated." "Perhaps
Perhaps I ought to have reasoned thus,
he replied, but I could not. I could
have freed not the knowledge would yet it did
not. I could not derive benefit

from the later knowledge of your character which I had acquired, I could not bring it into play; it was overwhelmed, buried, lost in those earlier feelings, which I had been smarting under year after year. I could think of you only as one who had yielded, ~~who had given~~ ~~~~ ~~~~ ~~~~ ~~~~ I saw you with the very person who had guided you in that year of misery. I had no reason to believe her of less authority now. — The force of habit was to be added. — "I should have thought," said Anne, "that my manner to you might have spared you much, or all of this." "No, no, your manner might be only the case, which your engagement to another man. ~~~~ I felt you with this belief. ~~~~ I was determined to see you again. ~~~~ My spirits rallied with the morning, & I felt that I had still a motive for remaining here. — The Admiral's news indeed, was a revulsion.

Since that moment, I have been ~~decided~~ ~~only for its confirmation~~ determined what to do — and had it been confirmed I ~~should have~~ would have ~~been~~ ~~left Bath that day in truth.~~ There was time for all this to pass &c——

The contents of this Drawer

for Anna

NOTES

NOTES TO CHAPTER 10

The variants cited on this chapter are
(1) from the MS.
(2) from the *Memoir*, second edition, 1871.
(3) for pp. 18–25, from the posthumous first edition, 1818, pp. 283–292 of the last volume.

Page 3

2. this authority to impart *for* with this power of imparting

   left *for* quitted
6. at Mr Elliot *over* about Mr Elliot (by what she had heard about *above line*) *erased*
8. Lady Russell] *A passage in erasure follows :* & glancing with composed Complacency & (*possibly* Lenient) Triumph upon the fact of her having been right & Lady R. wrong (herself *above line*) the most discriminating of the two. *She* had never been satisfied. Lady Russell's confidence had been entire. *All this is erased, except the words* confidence . . . entire, *which are retained with the insertion of* whose *before* confidence

   Over the earlier part of this is written: greiving with complacency or triumphing with concern that Events should (*several words doubtful*)
9. in him (*the second word is doubtful*) *added above line after* confidence

   The Embarrassment *for* But the Embarrassment
11. hour *for* moment

Page 4

2. Agitation *for* Embarrassment
3. it *erased after* the end of

NOTES

4. much engrossed *for* far engrossed
   that she started on *for* as to start at
6. he were *added above line before* a person
11. denied it *over* said *erased*
15. calling out *for* saying
16. she is all alone *added above line*
    & *erased before* in & rest
17. at this time to be in company of any sort, that it vexed her *for* for any company but that of her own thoughts, that she was really sorry
20. now *erased before* obliged
21. so *erased before* kind *and restored before* very
    said (cried *above line*) *erased and* said *restored*

Page 5

2. The possibility of Capt. W. had occurred—and most *over* She had Capt. W. in her thoughts at this moment; and ever *erased*
4. was she *added above line after* anxious
6. (but *erased*) *which*, might have been a question— *over* she could not have told *which* herself *erased*
8. but *over* by *erased after* Nobody
14. merely *erased after* allow me
15. be so good as to *added above line*
17. very happy *for* glad
18. Mind *added above line*

Page 6

2. you have not *for* I do not see
3. in your Countenance *erased after* Look of it
   as Grave as a little Judge *added above line*
5. all *erased before* right (that will do now, it is all right *1871*)
6. She *for* Anne
8. wild *added above line*
   disclosure *for* confession of the past

NOTES

11. how far more probable (it was *erased*) that he should *over* that it he must in all probability *erased (1871 retains* it was)
13. was *erased before* evidently
20. shall *erased before* will

Page 7

7. a Nobody] nobody *1871*
17. by the fire pretending to read & prepared for no greater surprise than *for* in the pretence of reading, & preparing to be surprised only by

Page 8

1. be quietly] to be quietly *1871*
2. to leave any troublesome pause *for* to leave them any troublesome pauses
4. about his wife & everybody *over* & he would go upstairs & give his wife notice *erased*
11. arose again—to entreat] arose, again to entreat *1871*
17. did not with a more passive Determination *for* with determined spirit

Page 9

3. but on reaching the door, said, *added above line*
5. when he (had *above line*) reached the door *erased after* please
6. and instantly, before they were well out of the room, the Adm¹ continued " As I am going to *over* & tho' they did both pass on to the Landing place & the Admiral beleived himself to be speaking low, she *erased*
9. fit *erased before* but fair
16. distinguish *for* hear
    for *for* as
18. any *added above line*
20. in an undertone *erased after* trying

NOTES

Page 10

1. she was very much distressed (disturbed *1871*) *for* It agitated her very much
4. possibility *for* danger
6. at all *added above line*
9. Lease *deleted after* Adm^ls *and restored*
10. something of *added above line*
11. or not signed *added above line*
13. but then followed *added above line*
17. wanting to be excused—wanting to put something off. " Phoo, Phoo—answered the Admiral *over* " but (*word illegible*) *erased*
21. speak myself *for* do it myself
    was the Adm^l's reply (answer *above line*) *erased after* myself
22. followed *erased after* impatience *and added above line*

Page 11

1. (who *erased*) opening (*corrected from* opened) *over* opening *erased*
3. (with *erased*) replied the Admiral, in all the power of his natural voice *for* met her eye ear, in all the strength of the Adm^l's voice
7. hastily *added above line*
   & *erased before* the door
13. and *added above line before* for about
18. but could only compass the *over* but she (& sought? *above line*) could only (*perhaps* secure) *erased*
19. of *for* in *after* releif
20. anxious, the *erased before* distressing

Page 12

1. a voice of effort & constraint *for* the voice of a Man who *would* speak whether he could or no
3. already *erased after* Madam *and added above line*

NOTES

4. the *erased before* Adm¹
5. some particular] a particular *1871*
7. do it *for* do so (*1871 retains* do so)
8. feelings *erased after* to my
12. only *added above line*
17. and *added above line before* You will perceive
18. that *om. 1871*

Page 13

3. very *erased before* forced
6. word] soul *1871*
7. really *erased before* ashamed
8. quick] quickly *1871*
9. sort] kind *1871*
17. knew *added above line*
22. his Lease of Kellynch *for* the Lease

Page 14

4. under *for* in
8. required to *erased before* commissioned
19. Pronounce (*originally* say ?) only the words,
    he may, *added above line*
    and *add. 1871 after* he may
21–page 15. 1. This was spoken . . . meet the message *om. 1871* (*by homoeoteleuton*)

Page 15

12. Power *for* brilliancy
13. possessed *for* could command
17. enjoying the releif *for* feeling the comfort
18. or *added above line before* of playing
20. & *added above line before* looked

Page 16

3. side *om. 1871*
7. the fullness] all the fullness *1871*
8. was *erased before* Suspense
20. hardly *added above line*
22. be *added above line before* very likely

NOTES

Page 17

3. a summons *for* some summons
7. set in *for* established
10. a note was dispatched to Camden Place *added above line*
11. she *erased before the second* staid
13. more than one interval was secured to them by Mrs. Croft *erased before* the Husband
17. gone *erased before* down *and before* upon
19. Landing place] landing *1871*
21. all *for* many of

Page 18

3. in the first place *added above line*
5. inexpressibly *added above line*
7. *From this point to p. 25, l. 16, the text of the MS. is largely identical with the posthumous print of 1818; variants are recorded here from sentences and phrases which are substantially the same, the wider divergences being ignored.*
8. maintaining *for* bearing
9. just] loveliest *1818*
11. & prefer *added above line*
13. any *erased before* Justice
14. his own sensations] himself *1818*; his own feelings *1871*
17. kind] sort *1818*
18. *roused (ital.)*] roused *(rom.) 1818*
21. *attempts (ital.)*] attempts *(rom.) 1818, 1871*

Page 19

1. Anger & Pique] angry pride *1818*
2. continually *for* ever
   the impossibility *for* an impossibility
3. Louisa *for* her
4. *that day (ital.)*] that day *(rom.) 1818*
6. tha *erased before* the Mind

NOTES

8. a comparison] *so 1818* ; comparison *1871*
   the unrivalled] unrivalled *1818*
9. his (him *above line*) *erased before* his own
17. begun] had begun *1871*
20. From that period his penance had become severe *1818*

Page 20

3. begun] had begun *1871*
4. had *repeated before* begun *and erased*
6–p. 21, l. 5. *This passage is converted in 1818 into direct speech.*
7. as an] an *1871*
12. instantly *over* to them *erased*
    yet *added above line before* made him feel
14. even *added above line after* herself
19. justly on this subject before—he had not *over* before of what his, as he ought, His leaving Lyme had been the consequence of never *all erased* (*1818 has* justly *for* seriously)
    he had] and he had *1871*

Page 21

5. too late] too late, in short *1818*
10. feelings] sentiments *1818*
14. *fair (ital.*)] fair (*rom.*) *1818*
15. sentiments] sentiment *1871* ; feelings *1818*
16. him] them *1871*
    and he went therefore into Shropshire *added above line* (to his brother's *1818*)
18. the Crofts at Kellynch] Kellynch *1818*
19. then *erased before* act
    as he found requisite] as circumstances might require *1818*
21. Blindness *for* blunders
    & *added above line before* the Blunders

NOTES

Page 22

1. Louisa *for* Uppercross
2. astonishing felicity] astonishing and felicitous intelligence *1818*
3. with Benwicke *for* to Benwicke
   Bath, Bath *for* To Bath, To Bath (*1871 prints* Bath—Bath had instantly followed)
6. at (*erased and restored*) the first sight *for* at the first re-appearance
9. this morning's] the morning's *1871*
12. *After* be capable of *is inserted the long passage beginning* He was very eager *and ending* (p. 25) *with* my last day in Bath. *This was written at the end of the manuscript; its position is ascertained by a × in the text and at the end of the manuscript, and by the repetition, in the latter place, of the succeeding words* There was Time for all this to pass, &c.
15. at the Concert *for* the Eveng before
19. appeating & (dividing her from him *erased*) tearing her away *over* appearance & of her being instantly lost to him *erased*
21. subsequent moments *for* other moments afterwards
22. Despondence (*originally* despair?) *for* alarm (despondènce *1871*)

Page 23

1. all *om. 1818, 1871*
   energy *for* the energy of Love
2. cried he *for* said he
3. *my* (*ital.*)] my (*rom.*) *1818, 1871*
5. conversing & smiling *added above line*
8. certain *for* probable
11. that *erased before* what
12. supports] support *1871*

NOTES

13. me *added above line after* fool of
    which my behaviour expressed] which I appeared *1818, 1871*
15. agony *for* feeling my extreme danger
16. *Friend (ital.)*] friend *(rom.) 1818, 1871*
18, 20. *had, Persuasion, once (ital.)*] had, persuasion, once *(rom.) 1818, 1871*
19. the indelible, immoveable Impression of *added above line*
20. of your *erased before* what

Page 24

2. was *added above line before* so different *and erased*
4. *was (ital.)*] was *(rom.) 1818, 1871*
5. that *om. 1871*
8. *Duty (ital.) twice*] duty *(rom.) 1818, 1871*
12. Perhaps I ought to have reasoned thus, he replied, but I could not *for* You are right —he cried—This ought to have weighed with me, but it did not
14. the later knowledge of your Character which I had acquired] the late knowledge I had acquired of your character *1818, 1871*
20. —who *had* yeilded, who *had* given me up, who *had* been influenced by any one rather than by *me*—(*had is italicized three times, all printed in roman in 1818 and 1871*)

Page 25

1. *me (ital.)*] me *(rom.) 1818, 1871*
4. think] believe *1818, 1871*
    now *added above line after* authority
7. yourself *for* you
11. would give *for* might produce
12. with this beleif] in this belief *1871*
    yet *added above line*
13. however *erased after* again

NOTES

18. been decided *over* waited only for its confirmation determined *erased*
    decided] divided *1871*
19. this (day *erased*) would have been my *last day* in Bath *for* I should have left Bath tomorrow
21. for *over* was *erased*
    pass *over* be said—& *erased*

Page 26

1. the communication *for* conversation
3. other two *over* more *erased*
   at once so *over* more *erased*
5. of *repeated and erased after* Sopha
9. & to endeavour to silence *erased after* satisfy
   as to *over* on the subject of his enquiry *erased*
10. innate *erased before* delicacy
11. good nature *for* good humour
17. indeed *om. 1871*
19. why should they have waited so long? *over* it w^d (must *above line*) have been done before now (long ago *above line*) *erased*
21. closed *over* was bef *over erased*

Page 27

1. (and *erased*) whose *over* the very *erased*
2. parting *for* which M^{rs} C— parted
3. gave *over* made *erased*
   beleive at least that *erased after* Anne
   persuasion of her seeing & *for* Beleif of her warmly
4. what she saw or conjectured *erased after* approving
9. looking back *for* reflecting on it
11. remainder *for* rest

NOTES TO CHAPTER 11

The variants cited on this chapter are
(1) from the MS.
(2) from the posthumous first edition, 1818, pp. 298-308 of the last volume.

Page 29

1. Who can want (to hear *above line*) anything further ? *erased before* Who can be
5. carry their point *for* bear down all opposition
11. a *added above line before* Capt. W—
12. fail *deleted after* Anne E— *and restored above line after* between them
14. one *for* an *before* Independant

Page 30

15. *after* Daughter *1818 adds* at present
19. his Daughter *for* Anne (*1818 has* Anne)
22. it *over* her *erased* (*see the note on the cancelled passage which immediately follows*).
    From a bad match *to* volume of Honour *is written on a scrap pasted on, which cancels (and partly obliterates) what was originally written. This was somewhat as follows :*
    a (to be making a *erased*) *bad* Match for her. As he saw (more of *erased*) & conversed with Capᵗ W. more, saw (him *erased*) his complexion by daylight—& conversed with him & perceived in (by such *erased*) e⟨on versa⟩tion that his Teeth ⟨were remark⟩ably fine (⟨as fine⟩ as ever *erased*)—he co⟨uld not⟩ but feel that in any (pre⟨sent⟩ *added above line*) ⟨compari⟩son with Anne, Capt. W. must have the advantage, that *he* had lost much less of Youth & bloom (since former days *erased*) than *she* had,

NOTES

and (that *erased*) consequently (he (*ital.*) *erased*) might now pretend to a much better (the best *above line*) Match than she could (of the two *above line*).

Page 31

2. saw him by daylight *erased after* Capt. W. (saw him repeatedly by daylight and eyed him well *1818*)
4. *his ... her* (*ital.*)] his ... her (*rom.*) *1818*
7. together *erased after* name *and added above line after* this (*1818 has* assisted by *for* together with)
10. the Marriage *over* F. W. Esqre Post-Capt. of H.M.'s Navy in his Bar chosen volume *erased*
11. person] one *1818*
12. feelings] feeling *1818*
    excite any serious anxiety *for* be any serious anxiety to them

Page 32

1. appearances in *for* the manners of
3. exact *erased before* ideas
9. suavity *erased before* general
13. for *erased before* less
17. *From* There is a quickness *to* than her young friend *is written between the lines of an erased passage ; some of the interlineations, however, belong to the cancelled and not to the substituted passage, so that restoration is not easy. The cancelled passage ran somewhat as follows :*
    Bad Morality again. A young Woman proved to have (had *above line*) more discrimination of Character than her elder—to have seen in two Instances more clearly what a Man was (it was about than her Godmother ! *above line*). But on the point of

NOTES

Morality, I confess myself almost in despair after understanding (myself *above line*) to have (already *above line*) given a Mother offence—having already appeared weak in the point where I thought myself most strong and shall leave it (leave the present matter *above line*) to the mercy of Mothers & Chaperons & Middle-aged Ladies in general

There *is* (*ital.*)] There is (*rom.*) *1818*

in some *added above line and erased after* in short

18. of Taste *erased after* nicety

Page 33

1. Lady R. *erased after* but she
2. very *added above line before* good
6. the awkwardness of the Beginning *for* the first awkwardness of Novelty
9. sort of *erased before* Mother
   who *over* whom she *erased*
   continually seeing *erased before* securing
10. the *over* that *erased before* happiness
    other *erased before* Child (*retained in 1818*)
12. by *over* when *erased before* the circumstance
14. and *added above line before* she might
15. that she had been] with having been *1818*
    she *over* it had been at *her* house, that it *erased*
16. the connection *for* it
17. having Anne staying with her] keeping Anne with her *1818*
    staying *for* to stay
20. to her *erased after* agreable

Page 34

2. into contact *for* to be together
5. *she . . . future* (*ital.*)] she . . . future (*rom.*) *1818*
8. a family *for* the family

NOTES

10. Knighted *erased before* made a Baronet
    she would not change situations with Anne *for* it would be all very well
12. *Eldest* (*ital.*)] eldest (*rom.*) *1818*
13. *her* (*ital.*)] her (*rom.*) *1818*
14. for a change is not very probable there *for* as a change of it is not very probable
19. *him* (*ital.*)] him (*rom.*) *1818*
21. unexpectedly *for* unwelcomely
    (unpleasantly *above line*) & was very unwelcome *erased after* unexpectedly

Page 35

1. hopes] hope *1818*
4. given (him *erased*) *over* put in his power *erased*
7. soon *added above line and* soon after *erased after* Bath
8. quitting it likewise soon afterwards *for* following him soon after
11. evident how double a Game (that *erased*) he had been playing (a double game *erased*) *over* pretty evident on what terms they had previously been *erased*
14. *one* (*ital.*)] one (*rom.*) *1818*
17. possibility *for* power
21. cunning *for* finesse
22. finally *for* ultimately
    There are Bets of her being still Lady Elliot at last *erased after* carry the day

Page 36

2. wheedled *for* teized
3. at last *added above line*
8. own *erased before* deception
   in her *for* as to her Character
9. to be sure *for* in Laura Place
   resort *for* turn

NOTES

12. themselves] in turn *1818*
13. is *for* was
15. *meaning (ital.)*] meaning (*rom.*) *1818*
22. keenly *over* keenness *erased*

Page 37

2. moment's *added above line*
8. to her feel Mind of Upright Delicacy *erased after* lively pain
9. her Mind *for* it
12. independant of himself, whom she *erased after* World
13. Lady R. *erased before* To those
19. have been *for* be
    originally *added above line*
20. almost *added above line before* anything
22. agreableness *erased before* claims

Page 38

4. their marriage, instead of depriving her *over* instead of being deprived *erased*
5. by Anne's (the *above line*) marriage, it gained her another *erased before* secured
6. When they had any home, she was frequently w *erased before* She was one
   one of their first visitors] their earliest visitor *1818*
9. her Husband's *for* the
10. giving her the *erased before* writing
    & acting] acting *1818*
14. friend *erased before* Man
15. convinced her of his being much nearer Perfection than her intercourse with the World had *erased before* fully requited
    she had rendered] which she had rendered *1818*
16. ever *added above line before* meant
    her friend *erased after* render

NOTES

7. *after* to his Wife *follows:*
   And having received such a benefit (*originally* frequent?) from him, not (?) even his wife could Mrs Smith's estimate of his Perfection could be surpassed only by that Wife's *over* and could not fail of establishing his And having done so much for her, scarcely could his wife even think him nearer perfection, —*both versions heavily erased. Then follows:*
   Finis. July 16. 1816
   which is also erased.
18. *spoiled* (*ital.*)] spoiled (*rom.*) *1818*
19. with *added above line after* Income
22. Activity] alacrity *1818*

Page 39

1. those] these *1818*
6. *Her* (*ital.*)] Her (*rom.*) *1818*
9. Anne *for* Anne's
10. the full *for* all the
13. *that* (*ital.*)] that (*rom.*) *1818*
14. dim *for* overspread
18. not more distinguished *erased before* if possible
19. in it's *for* for *before* Domestic *and before* National
20. Importance *for* Renown

LT   R/M 103KK
  WW
         AUSTEN